Phonics FUN
BOOK FIVE

The WITCH Had an ITCH

Short Vowel Sounds with Consonant Digraphs

Brian P. Cleary

Illustrations by **Jason Miskimins**

Consultant:
Alice M. Maday
PhD in Early Childhood Education with a Focus in Literacy
Assistant Professor, Retired
Department of Curriculum and Instruction
University of Minnesota

Lerner Publications ◆ Minneapolis

Lerner Publications Company
An imprint of Lerner Publishing Group, Inc.
241 First Avenue North
Minneapolis, MN 55401 USA

For reading levels and more information, look up this title at www.lernerbooks.com.

Main body text set in Mikado. Typeface provided by HVD.

Library of Congress Cataloging-in-Publication Data

Names: Cleary, Brian P., 1959– author. | Miskimins, Jason, illustrator. | Maday, Alice M., consultant.
Title: The witch had an itch : short vowel sounds with consonant digraphs / Brian P. Cleary ; illustrations by Jason Miskimins ; consultant: Alice M. Maday.
Description: Minneapolis : Lerner Publications , [2022] | Series: Phonics fun | Audience: Ages 4–8. | Audience: Grades K–1. | Summary: "The thing on the wing can sing. With rhyming, carefully leveled text and comedic, colorful illustrations, this book provides plenty of examples of short vowel sounds with consonant digraphs and encourages readers to try the sounds for themselves"– Provided by publisher.
Identifiers: LCCN 2021032470 (print) | LCCN 2021032471 (ebook) | ISBN 9781728441290 (library binding) | ISBN 9781728448527 (paperback) | ISBN 9781728444925 (ebook)
Subjects: LCSH: English language—Vowels—Juvenile literature. | English language—Consonants—Juvenile literature. | English language—Phonetics—Juvenile literature. | Reading—Phonetic method—Juvenile literature.
Classification: LCC PE1157 .C58 2022 (print) | LCC PE1157 (ebook) | DDC 428.1/3—dc23

LC record available at https://lccn.loc.gov/2021032470
LC ebook record available at https://lccn.loc.gov/2021032471

Manufactured in the United States of America
2-53298-49743-5/2/2022

Dear Parents and Educators,

As a former adult literacy coach and the father of three children, I know that learning to read isn't always easy. That's why I developed **Phonics Fun**—a series that employs a combination of devices to help children learn to read. This book uses rhyme, repetition, illustration, and phonics to introduce young readers to short vowel sounds and consonant digraphs—letter combinations that come together to form a new sound. These include combinations such as *ch*, *sh*, and *th*. Words in bold all feature short vowel sounds and consonant digraphs.

The bridge to literacy is one of the most important we will ever cross. It's my hope that the Phonics Fun series will help new readers to hop, gallop, and skip from one side to the other!

Sincerely,

Brian P. Cleary

Note to Readers

This book is all about short vowel sounds and consonant digraphs. You can hear them in words like **rock** and **sing**. The **bold** words in this book have short vowel sounds and consonant digraphs. They also rhyme!

clock

rock

4

Knock on the **rock** by the **clock.**

The **thing** on the **wing** can **sing**.

The **witch** in the **ditch** began to **itch.**

The **long song** was all **wrong.**

The **tack** is **back** on the **black rack**.

Chuck and the **duck** are **stuck** in the **muck.**

duck

14

Check the **speck** by the **wreck** on the **deck**.

wreck

Pack the **snack** in a **sack** from the **stack**.

The **bunch** has a **hunch** that they will **munch** and drink **punch** at **lunch**.

lunch

Make Your Own

Use the words on these pages to write a story with short vowel sounds and consonant digraphs!

rock

sing

witch

duck

wing

clock

trash

chip

ship

chin

dock

ash

Poet, literacy enthusiast, and word nerd **Brian P. Cleary** "grew up" in one of the largest creative divisions in the world, where he has put words in the mouths of Dolly Parton, William Shatner, and Kevin Nealon. He has written many best-selling grammar and poetry books for young readers.

Jason Miskimins graduated from the Columbus College of Art & Design in 2003. He works as an illustrator of books and greeting cards.

Alice M. Maday has a master's degree in early childhood education from Butler University and a PhD in early childhood education, with a focus on literacy, from the University of Minnesota. Her research interests include kindergarten curriculum, emergent literacy, parent and teacher expectations, and the place of preschool in the reading readiness process.